FOURTH MAN IN THE FIRE

By Edwin Yarsiah Forkpa
With Judith M. Bentley

Insignia
PUBLICATIONS

Sacramento, California

Fourth Man In The Fire

By Edwin Yarsiah Forkpa
With Judith Bentley

Copyright 2005 by Bentley Educational Ministries

All Scriptures are from the King James Version of the Bible

Published by Bentley Educational Ministries
11375 Northview Drive
Dexter, MO 63841

Printed in the United States
By Insignia Publications
Sacramento, CA
877.413.1100

Cover Design by Paul Povolni
Text Design by Dennis Fiorini

Insignia Publications
Sacramento, California
877.413.1100

FOURTH MAN
IN THE
FIRE

By Edwin Yarsiah Forkpa
With Judith M. Bentley

*With gratitude
to our editorial staff:*

Joyce Moore

Robert Bentley

Albert Stewart

Melanie Nordstrom

Kristin Hoover

*With deepest respect we dedicate
this book to—*

*Reverend Albert Stewart and family
who risked their lives for
the cause of Christ during the
Liberian Civil War*

&

*to God
For His faithfulness in preserving our lives
in the time of trouble.*

600 - 284 - 3100

Contents

Edwin Yarsiah Forkpa

Missing and Presumed Dead

It was the year of 1991 when I visited with Missionary Albert Stewart at a church conference. Reverend Stewart was the Superintendent of the United Pentecostal Church of Liberia. His anointed ministry coupled with his authoritative voice and physical bearing had blessed people world wide. He was a witness to the miraculous intervention of God during the time of the Civil War in Liberia. At the time of our conversation, the war was still raging.

"And what has happened to our friend Edwin Yarsiah?" I questioned Brother Stewart. Edwin had been a student of mine at Gateway College of Evangelism in the year of 1980. I knew him to be a gifted young preacher with an excellent spirit.

"Ah yes, Edwin Yarsiah," Missionary Stewart replied with a great sadness clouding his expression. "He is like a son to me. He has been caught in the middle of the Liberian Civil War. No one has heard from him for over a year now. We can only presume that he is dead."

My husband and I joined others who were praying that Edwin Yarsiah would indeed be found alive and that God himself would protect him from the fiery trial he would surely be experiencing if he was still alive.

Months later we would learn the story. Divine intervention had pre-empted our presumptions. Not dead—just walking through the fire. As with the three Hebrew children in Daniel chapter 3, at each stage of Edwin Yarsiah's frightening wartime saga, the fourth man was always present, protecting, delivering, and doing the miraculous.

The story is a modern day thriller. Read and be blessed.

Author Judy Bentley

3

A Fiery Message 1

I slipped the cassette into the tape deck and pushed the play button. As I leaned back in my chair in my home in Liberia, I heard the distinctive voice of a renowned preacher from America. The message of Tom Fred Tenney began ministering to my soul.

The message was entitled, "My Faith Fights For Me."

Now fighting was the furthest thing from my mind. If there was to be a fight, I wanted out. I was a preacher of the Gospel of Jesus Christ. My feet were shod with the Gospel of peace. My job was to preach and teach and baptize and pray.

The voice of preacher Tenney continued to echo in my ears.

Faith is the dynamite of the soul.

God can operate in the realm of thought, but faith is a flash of action.

There is a difference between faith and miracles. A miracle would have put out the fiery furnace for the three Hebrew lads. But faith took them in it while it burned.

A miracle would have killed the lions in Daniel's den, but faith kept him in their midst while they lived.

4

What we need is faith to live in these crises times. Faith to abide in these crises times. Faith to let our lights shine before men that they may see our good works and glorify our father which is in heaven.

The message stirred me deeply. I recalled how God had allowed those three Hebrew boys to be thrust into the fire because they would not bow to the idols of this world. But when the smoke died down, their victory was apparent. (Daniel 3:24-30)

Then Nebuchadnezzar the king was astonied, and rose up in haste, and spake, and said unto his counsellors, Did not we cast three men bound into the midst of the fire? They answered and said unto the king, True, O king.

*He answered and said, Lo, I see four men loose, walking in the midst of the fire, and they have no hurt; and **the form of the fourth is like the Son of God.***

Then Nebuchadnezzar came near to the mouth of the burning fiery furnace, and spake, and said, Shadrach, Meshach, and Abednego, ye servants of the most high God, come forth, and come hither. Then Shadrach, Meshach, and Abednego, came forth of the midst of the fire.

And the princes, governors, and captains, and the king's counsellors, being gathered together, saw these men, upon whose bodies the fire had no power, nor was an hair of their head singed, neither were their coats changed, nor the smell of fire had passed on them.

Then Nebuchadnezzar spake, and said, Blessed be the God of Shadrach, Meshach, and Abednego, who hath sent his angel, and delivered his servants that trusted in him, and have changed the king's word, and yielded their bodies, that they might not serve nor worship any god, except their own God.

Therefore I make a decree, That every people, nation, and language, which speak any thing amiss against the God of Shadrach, Meshach, and Abednego, shall be cut in pieces, and their houses shall be made a dunghill: because there is no other God that can deliver after this sort.

Then the king promoted Shadrach, Meshach, and Abednego, in the province of Babylon.

After listening intently to the powerful message, I filed it away in the back of my mind under the category of *"Great Messages I Have Heard."* How could I have known that danger was imminent? In a matter of days, I would be thrust into a horror like I had never experienced before. My family would be surrounded by death and destruction of the worst kind.

Yet in the midst of it all, it was this message of T. F. Tenney that would speak to me through the dark night of my soul and would give me courage to face the fears that lie ahead. I would not be delivered *from* the fire, but I would be victorious *in* the fire.

And always hovering nearby, there would be the shadow of the Fourth Man—guiding, protecting, and delivering.

8

9

The Moving Snail 2

The news of the Liberian civil conflict spread slowly, like a moving snail. We were used to tribal skirmishes. Liberia had experienced many uprisings that would last one or two months and then things would return to normal. And so, when fighting broke out, we summed it all up by thinking it was business as usual.

Most of the Christians in Liberia knew nothing about the war. Sometimes our lack of knowledge about such things made us careless. Carelessness can be tragic.

Since we as Christians were not in anyone's way and since the war was not against the Christian faith, we assumed we were safe.

From Butuwo to Kanplay, the snail moved slowly, receiving little resistance from the national army. In less than seven months, the war had closed in on us.

Missionaries from various denominations were closing their mission stations and leaving, but the national government, through its persuasive information machinery, continued to assure us that it was still capable of protecting us.

By December of 1989, an atmosphere of tension hung over the capital city of Monrovia. Samuel Doe had barricaded himself inside the executive palace while his forces fought to keep control of the city. The tension rose to the point of desperation. Like a dry season thunderstorm gathering rain clouds, we knew that the unrest would soon reach its saturation point. It would be just a matter of time. A spirit of fear and uncertainty infected the air.

Christmas that year was just a matter of formality for our family of five. There was no money for buying gifts or festive foods. My wife Ellen and I and our three sons, Edwin, Christian, and Elijah were living at a bare subsistence level. It was a somber time for all of us.

Clear evidence of the approaching war was seen everywhere. Supermarket shelves were quickly becoming empty, major stores were closing, prices rose sky high, and transportation fares became unaffordable for most people.

As Christmas of 1989 passed, a new decade was ushered in—a decade in which all Liberia would shake hands with one of the bloodiest civil wars in the history of Africa.

12

13

History

On December 24, 1989, a struggle for leadership began in the West African country of Liberia. Charles Taylor led the National Patriotic Front of Liberia (NPFL) in an effort to overthrow Samuel Doe, the cruel dictator who had ruled the country since 1980. By 1990, Taylor's forces controlled most of the country but had not been able to take the capital city of Monrovia where Doe was holding out in the executive palace.

The warring factions were divided between ethnic lines. They were further complicated by a split that year between Taylor and Prince Johnson. Johnson led the Gio tribe. Taylor led the large Mano tribe (and some Gios who were loyal to him), and Doe's forces consisted mainly of the Krahn and Mandingo tribes. Neighboring West African countries sent in a peacekeeping force to try to bring order to Liberia. Taylor resisted.

In September 1990, Prince Johnson's small band captured, tortured, and killed Doe. The leader of Doe's presidential guard, General David Nimblay, assumed the leadership of Doe's supporters. His fighters were called the United Liberation Movement of Liberia for Democracy. A stalemate set in, with all three factions vying for control.

After six devastating years of fighting, a peace plan was signed in 1996. 200,000 civilians died during the looting and killing rampages by the various militias, and some by starvation. It was one of the bloodiest civil wars in the history of the continent of Africa.

Voinjama

Zorzor

LOFA

Yekepa

Noway Camp

Sanniquellie

GRAND
CAPE
MOUNT

Gahnpa
(Ghanta)

Gbarnga

Palala

BONG

NIMBA

Bong Town

Totota

nanburg

Kle

BOMI

MARGIBI

MONTSERRADO

Kakata

Tapeta

Monrovia

Gardnersville

Paynesville

GRAND
BASSA

Harbel

RIVER
CESS

Zwedru

Buchanan

GRAND GEDEH

Pyne
Town

River
Cess

SINOE

Liberia

Greensville

GRAND
KRU

Nyaaka

Barclayville

Plibo

Grand
Cess

Harper

NORTH
ATLANTIC
OCEAN

15

The Taste of Fear 3

I woke up early one Monday morning, feeling quite confused. I felt my way in the darkness toward the living room. I wanted to pray.

I was working as the director of the Presbyterian Todee Mission School, located three miles outside the city of Kakata. I had been hired to be the administrator of this school in the absence of the principal who had traveled to America.

When I assumed this position, the place was in a state of disrepair. In conjunction, the morale of the staff and the students was at an all time low. I worked hard to restore order to the school, but the changes I enacted were not well received. This adverse reaction was partly due to the fact that I was a Pentecostal preacher giving orders in a Presbyterian school.

After much uproar and many conflicts, I finally succeeded in bringing some order to the chaos. In my heart I knew, however, that I was very much out of step with God's purposes for my life.

That Monday morning I began to pray. "Oh, Lord, if there's a lingering danger that I don't know about, please keep me and my family and all these students safe from danger." I had difficulty keeping my mind focused while I prayed. Finally I left the room and joined my family as we prepared for the day's work.

By the time I finished dressing, the sun was rising slowly above the tall rubber trees that circled the mission station. I rushed into my office feeling all the time that something was terribly wrong.

Fear gripped us as we heard the news of the advancing rebel warriors closing in on us. Throughout the week, frightened parents began arriving at the mission station, asking to take their children home.

"Why do you want to take your children home? They need to be in school," I insisted.

Each parent concocted a different excuse and none of my pleadings seemed to affect their decisions. The atmosphere at the mission station was filled with uncertainty.

After meeting with the teachers, it was decided that the wisest course of action would be to close the mission school for two weeks to see what would develop. Soon we received a visit from the mission supervisor. By now, all signs of danger were clearly visible. She agreed that closing the school was the best course of action, but requested that we visit the nearby Todee Military Academy to see if we could get some helpful information.

Saturday morning we went to the military academy only to find out that events were pretty well out of control. There were almost no soldiers in sight except for a few guards who appeared very frightened when they saw us.

The soldiers from the government camp assured us that all was well and that there was nothing to be afraid of. These armed forces of Liberian soldiers, probably knew that we didn't believe their propaganda because they kept asking us, "Are you people afraid of the rebels?"

We returned to our mission station and began making plans to transport the remaining students to their homes.

That same day, we received a visit from a brother in the Lord, John C. Mulbah. "Brother Yarsiah, I think it would be good to take your three sons away from here as soon as possible. With your permission, I will take them to Kakata where they should be safe. After all your students have left, you can join us there this evening."

"Yes, Brother Mulbah, that seems like a very good idea," my wife and I agreed. "We'll see you shortly."

Ellen hurriedly packed a few things for the kids. We hugged them, and bade them a quick good-by as we returned to our responsibilities at the school. The city of Kakata was only three miles away and we were quite sure our family would be reunited at the end of the day.

Hurriedly we returned to the task of taking the children to their homes. We arranged for the first group of students to leave in a Jeep with a four wheel drive, that belonged to one of the supervisors. We then loaded my Toyota Corolla with as many students as it could possibly hold. Ellen and I and the other teachers were scheduled to leave on the next trip. The rest of the day we waited anxiously, but much to our distress, the cars never returned.

Homeless

Early Sunday morning the national radio station, ELBC, announced: "Kakata has fallen to the forces of the National Patriotic Front of Liberia." This announcement confirmed our worst fears. We were forced to make a quick decision.

We began walking the three mile distance to Kakata on foot. We still had around ten of our students with us and one of the teachers. Adding to our difficulties, Ellen was in the third month of pregnancy, expecting our fourth child.

As we approached the city, we came to a roadblock. One of the guards called out, "You can't go any further than this. The rebels have seized the city of Kakata." All roads to Kakata were closed to traffic of any kind.

We could hear the echo of machine guns in the distance. The city was on fire. People were being killed and their houses burned to the ground.

What could we do? Where were our sons? Would we ever see them again? Ellen began sobbing.

What was to become of our family? We could do nothing to remedy the tragic situation. Our fate was in the hands of God.

20

We were forced to make another quick decision. We started the long walk to Monrovia, a distance of forty-two miles.

To compound our problems, some of the students had a serious attack of malaria and they were showing signs of weakness. One of the boys began vomiting and we continually had to stop and try to help him. This slowed our trip down considerably.

In order to avoid contact with the fighters, we were forced to take several bypasses. In one of the small villages along the way, we came across some of the Todee Mission School students who lived there.

"Where are your children?" they questioned Ellen. My wife began to weep as she told them of the uncertainty of their whereabouts or their safety. Frustrated, confused, and homeless, we continued walking to Monrovia, not knowing whether our boys were dead or alive.

By the time we reached the paved road, the highway was completely clear. All traffic had been cut off. The only moving vehicles in sight were the army Jeeps with a few uniformed AFL soldiers cursing loudly at the rebels who were nowhere in sight.

We took the remaining students to their various homes and entered the capital city of Monrovia. The Lord provided a temporary residence for us on Duport Road at the home of a church friend, Ruby Koisee. This dear lady and her husband had a large family to feed and care for, but welcomed us in spite of the inconvenience.

By this time the airwaves were hot with news of the advancing warriors. Some newspapers even stated that the rebels would not die, no matter how many times they were shot at. Reports like this caused a wave of fear to grip us.

To add to our already agitated spirit of apprehension, BBC announced that every American citizen or foreigner residing in Liberia, should prepare to vacate immediately. The American government even decided to help a few Liberians leave for the USA.

We prayed that God would stop the war, but it was not to be. God had his own plan for us, even far greater than we could ever imagine.

"God where are you?" I prayed.

"I didn't move," came God's answer. "I'm still where I always was. I still rule heaven and earth. I hold the keys to death, hell, and the grave. I will not save you *from* this war. I will save you *in* this war."

Psalm 46:9-10

He maketh war to cease
unto the end of the earth,
he breaketh the bow
and cutteth the spear in sunder,
he burneth the chariot in the fire.
Be still and
know that I am God.

S.O.S.

In the midst of the horrifying situation all around us, I sat down and penned a letter to my American friend, Sister Joyce Moore whom I often referred to as my mother in the Lord.

May 29, 1990

Dear Sister Moore:
Greetings in the lovely name of our Lord and Savior, Jesus Christ, from whom all blessings flow.

"God is our refuge and strength, a very present help in trouble. Therefore will we not fear, though the earth be removed. . ." (Psalm 46:1,2).

I am writing not to frighten you, but rather to inform you that we are caught between life an death. Liberia, our once peace loving land where other people once sought peace and freedom, is now a war zone. We are under heavy rebel attack from almost every side. The government forces are trying to maintain peace and order, but up to now, there has been no positive result.

On Sunday, May 27, 1990, I fled with my family out of the Mission Station where we have been working since last year. Earlier on Saturday, May 26, 1990, I sent my three sons, Edwin Yarsiah, Jr., Christian, and Elijah with a brother from our church to wait for us in Kakata with the hope that my wife and I would follow later.

24

That night we could not join the boys in Kakata for lack of transportation and therefore had to spend the night without them. That night there was a heavy attack on Kakata City where our boys were. The next morning, Ellen and I tried to go to Kakata to find our boys, but security officers stopped us saying that there were heavy fightings going on in Kakata and that all roads leading to Kakata were blocked.

We therefore fled to Monrovia to seek help to get our children out. We are presently in Monrovia without our three children. We came to Monrovia with absolutely nothing. No change of clothes, no sufficient money to buy food or to rent a room in the city—all of these in the absence of our three precious boys. What a feeling!

Please contact other friends of ours in America to pray for us. The Stewarts and other United Pentecostal Church members are very much in a state of uncertainty as to the outcome of all of these troubles. Only prayers can save us now. Will America pray for Liberia?

Please use the address I gave you to transfer any financial assistance to us as fast as possible and advise us as you see fit.

Bye-bye now Mom. I love you so much and you know I miss you.

> *Love in Christ,*
> *Edwin and family*

25

Monrovia on Fire

As soon as we arrived in Monrovia, I contacted Brother Albert Stewart, our church superintendent, and my father in the Lord. The occasion was one that was tension-packed. Monrovia was now shaking with great uncertainty.

"Brother Stewart, what are we going to do?" I questioned.

"To be frank with you, Brother Edwin, I don't know. I just don't know."

Little did I realize that would be the last time I would see Brother Stewart for years to come. In two weeks time, Monrovia would be under heavy fire.

As I walked away to go back to Duport Road, I noticed that the streets were empty. I sensed an approaching danger. I knew that it would be just a matter of time until something disastrous would happen. I felt helpless against the forces all around me. There was nothing I could do except to pray for God's divine intervention.

It was on a Sunday morning that we found ourselves lying flat on our face on the floor of our house, trying to escape any stray bullet that might come our way. The house we were in was constructed of zinc, while most of the other homes were made of concrete. To our amazement, not one bullet hit that house. Many of the surrounding homes were hit and many people were killed and wounded even though their houses were made of concrete.

In spite of the danger, many of us braved the storm to attend service at the Sinker United Pentecostal Church where I had been asked to preach. The message God gave me for that service was, "This Storm Will End in a Great Calm," taken from Luke the eighth chapter.

We sang and prayed and worshiped with all of our hearts. The service was greatly blessed by God. We had no way of knowing that it would be years before we would be able to worship together again.

I remember seeing Sister Else Lund at that service. Sister Lund was dean of Maranatha Bible Institute in Monrovia. We often referred to her as Mother West Africa. She had given many years to ministering in our country and we respected her greatly.

That Sunday morning I remember expressing my fears to her concerning the whereabouts of our three boys. Sister Lund took time to encourage me. "The Lord will take care of them, Brother Yarsiah," she assured me. That was the last time that I saw Sister Lund.

To our amazement, before the end of the service, one of the saints arrived with good news. Our boys were alive and well in the town of Bong Mines! God had preserved their lives in the midst of the disastrous killing and burning that had taken place in Kakata.

I left that service greatly uplifted in the Lord. That would be the service and the message we would long remember: "This storm will end in a great calm." How long the storm would last, the Lord did not say. That was His secret and He chose not to reveal it to us at that time.

With the increasing insecurity in the country, the American Embassy sounded one last warning, advising all its citizens to leave Liberia. Brother Stewart, accompanied by several national board members, took Sister Else Lund to the airport for the last flight that would be leaving from Monrovia.

When they arrived at the airport, they saw many Liberians there who were begging and pleading to board the airplane, even if they had to sit on the floor. Nevertheless, Missionary Albert Stewart was offered an opportunity to leave on that last plane. He had already sent his wife and one of his children to America on a prior flight. He and six of his children remained in Liberia.

"Elder, are you leaving us?" the board members questioned him with sadness in their voices.

"No, I can't leave you here like this. How could I do that?" he answered. Brother Stewart chose to stay in Liberia with his six children. He has the heart of a true shepherd who never abandons his flock in the time of trouble.

A week went by rather quickly. By this time, most of the banks and main offices in Monrovia were completely shut down for security purposes and most people were staying inside their homes. Occasionally someone would venture out, in hopes of finding food.

July 10th, 1990 is a date I will never forget. An expectant mother knocked on Sister Koisee's door early in the morning. She was about to give birth to her baby. Since Ruby Koisee was a nurse, the lady pleaded with her. "Will you please help me? My baby is coming and I'm very frightened."

And so it was that on that fateful day, a new child was born in the house where we were staying. My wife assisted in the delivery of the baby.

As soon as the baby arrived, there was a bomb blast in the area. Everyone began running helter skelter. As we fled out of the yard, Sister Koisee grabbed the mother by the hand and we ran across an open field leading to the main highway. There was also a blind lady in the house who was a member of our church. We grabbed a wheelbarrow, put her in it, and carried her with us. The scene was a nightmare.

I vividly remember the scenes as all hell broke loose on the city of Monrovia. It was like a terrible hurricane, leveling everything in its path. The fighting reached all the way to the main city center.

We fled for our lives, with bullets flying all around us. I had arisen early, so I was fully dressed, but the rest of our group was still in their night clothes. We ran as hard as we could, trying our best to stay together. The war had reached a critical stage and we could expect nothing less than the worst.

As we left the area where we had been residing, a yard dog followed us down the road. Upon seeing a pack of dogs, it jumped into a fight with one of them. A soldier came by and shot the yard dog while the rest of the dogs fled in terror. The thought struck me that the dog would probably be used for the soldier's next meal, since food was so scarce.

Fear reigned supreme on that terrible day we will never forget.

The Albert Stewart Family

31

32

33

Death Valley 7

We joined more than 10,000 people exiting Monrovia on the road to Kakata. Most of them were walking with their belongings on their heads. Some rolled wheelbarrows carrying their elderly folks. It was a sight to behold.

By this time the government troops were attacking the NPFL just a short distance away. We found ourselves being sandwiched between the two fighting forces.

As we pushed into a nearby yard to catch our breath, we saw two elderly people inside a house. They were apparently unaware that everyone had evacuated the area.

We were forced to make a quick decision. We concluded that the best thing to do was to force the newborn baby and his mother into the house with the old folks, so we could continue our journey. I never found out what happened to that mother and her child who did not have the blessing of a father during that terrible time of war.

We approached the main highway with our hands held above our heads to show that we were civilians and not a part of the fighting forces. The sights around us were gruesome. We were stepping over corpses lying all along the road. Some of the bodies were already decomposed. Then we saw a sight that disturbed us even more. Down the road about a block from where we stood, we saw Superintendent Stewart's jeep leaning on one side with

34

all the tires removed. As I stared at the looted car, a hundred thoughts flashed through my confused mind. Apparently the fighters had killed our dear Brother Stewart and his children.

As we walked through this valley of death, we began to hear the loud voices of people coming from the nearby Omega Tower where about 50,000 people had gathered. Later we were to find out that those who went that direction had undergone a very critical screening. Many of them were killed and never made it to safety.

Just ahead of us walked a white gentleman wearing nothing by shorts. He was chain smoking as he stumbled down the road. I was told that he was the manager of the Coca-Cola factory which was just a block ahead of us.

The main highway itself was deserted with only a few armed men walking in combat formation. Other fighters were taking position under the tables in an abandoned market place. One of them shouted to us, "Keep right on the main highway and move on. Do not hold your hands up like that. You are not prisoners of war. Hurry and leave. We don't want the government forces to kill you and blame it on us."

We were forced to go through inspections at various rebel gates. At one of the gates, one of the rebels called out to me, "Do you know who I am?"

I thought it was best not to show fear, so instead of answering him, I simply smiled. He became incensed at this, and rushed toward me screaming, "Am I looking funny to you?" And with that, he stuck a long knife under my throat. "I think I will kill you right here and now." After a few minutes he changed his mind and let me continue down the road. From that moment on I knew we were in for real trouble.

We finally arrived at the junction of the road leading to the Omega Tower, along with thousands of others. The fighters from the NPFL were very much in charge of things. They were inspecting people's belongings and asking for their names and tribes. Checkpoints lined the routes.

A soldier came past us dragging a man whom he accused of belonging to one of the tribes opposing the aim of the fighters. Before the man could tell him that he was not of that tribe, the soldier shot him and pushed him into a ditch by the roadside. His lifeless body fell headlong into the ditch.

Before we knew what happened, one of the soldiers grabbed Sister Koisee's husband and dragged him away from our group, threatening to kill him. This sent our little group of Apostolic Pentecostals into a state of disarray. Our friend, Ruby Koisee, fainted and had to be carried to safety. "Just leave me here and let me die," she cried out.

"No, Sister Koisee, we can't do that. We've got to trust the Lord that He will help us." I managed to keep her encouraged by constantly quoting a Scripture in her ears: "Yea though I walk through the valley of the shadow of death, I will fear no evil for thou art with me."

36

As we moved down a small hill, we were ordered to walk in single file for inspection and identification. Some people were being called out of the line for investigation. At times, arguments broke out among the men sitting under the small thatched roof, interrogating all of us. They often disagreed among themselves. This delayed the entire process.

My wife Ellen was five months pregnant by this time. Elsie, my sister-in-law, was a few yards ahead of us. We were all in a state of distress, not knowing when death would come.

At the side of the road lay the decomposed body of a huge man. Apparently, the rain and sunshine made the man's exposed body look white, although it was actually the body of an elderly black man.

Suddenly, a man at the check point ahead of us called Elsie aside and demanded: "You are of the Krahn tribe, aren't you?"

"No, no, I am not of that tribe," Elsie insisted. "I am of the Belle tribe."

"You look like a Krahn girl to me," he insisted. "Look how fat you are. You people have been enjoying good food, right? If you don't tell the truth, we will kill you."

At that, the man seized her plait of hair and threw her on the ground. "With whom are you traveling?" he screamed at her. We looked on helplessly.

37

"I am with my sister and husband," she replied pointing to us as we arrived on the scene.

"Is that your sister?" the man directed his question to my pregnant wife, Ellen.

Ellen nodded. He further demanded, "Tell me the name of your tribe."

"We are all of the Belle tribe and we are from Lofa County," Ellen answered.

"Where is your husband?" he demanded. Ellen pointed to me with a frightened look in her eyes.

"All right, you two may leave," he pointed to the two women. "But this man will stay. We are going to kill him."

My wife tried to plead with the man on my behalf, but it was to no avail. "Keep moving. This man will speak for himself," the soldier answered her.

Ellen and Elsie stepped a few yards away from the main place of action and hid behind a small bush to see what would happen.

"Mister, what is your name?" he started. I looked him straight in the eye trying not to show fear, and I told him: "My name is Edwin Yarsiah."

"What tribe do you belong to?"

"I am of the Belle tribe and my home is Lofa County," I answered.

"What is the difference between the Belle people and the Krahn people?" he snarled. "You are all the same people. Isn't it true that you are not to see one another's blood?"

At this statement, I knew the intensity of the whole argument. I concluded that this man knew a whole lot about the traditional ties binding the two tribes together.

"My friend," I replied, "I don't know what you mean by that. All I know is that I am a Belle man from Lofa County and as you know, there is a great geographical difference between these two tribes."

"I do not believe you," he snapped. "Take off your shirt and your shoes. I believe you are a soldier for the government." He inspected my feet hoping to find some boot marks as clues. My socks were a bit tight and had left marks on my feet. "See there," he declared, "those are boot marks. You're one of the fighters."

Then one of the soldiers came from behind and hit me so hard on the chest that I nearly fell over.

When my interrogator failed in his attempt to prove me guilty, he simply announced, "We are going to kill you." In my mind at that moment, I was preparing to die. I grieved silently for my wife and children I would have to leave behind. Ellen and Elsie watched in terror from a distance.

39

My interrogator spoke to his superior. "What shall I do with this one?"

"Kill him!" came the reply. I looked toward the back of the building where they were executing people.

Suddenly a man stepped forward. I do not know who he was or where he came from. I have always believed him to be *The Fourth Man in the Fire.*

"Do you have any identification on you?" the man asked me.

"Yes I do," I said reaching into my pocket to take out my work identification card. I handed the card to this man.

Many of the fighters were illiterate, but I noticed that this man knew how to read. The man read the I. D. and then turned to my interrogator. "This card says Reverend Edwin Yarsiah. Why are you bothering this man? He is a man of God and these are not the people we are looking for." Then he turned to me. "Put on your clothes and go!"

I grabbed my clothes, but I didn't take time to put them on. I just began running. Suddenly, one of the men aimed an AK-47 at me and pulled the trigger. I kept running. The bullet whizzed by me as I went flying past the road block that the fighters had erected.

In a few seconds I was face to face with a very surprised Ellen. She thought I had been shot and was rushing to where she thought my body was. "Are you hurt?" she cried out to me.

"No, no, I am fine," I assured her. "God has sent an angel to protect me from death." It was a joyous moment for us, but there was no time to waste.

We hurried away while other soldiers were calling us to report to their side of the road. "Don't pay any attention to them," Ellen said. "We will lose ourselves in the crowd."

As we hurried down the road, we rejoiced together and thanked God for preserving my life as we walked through the valley of the shadow of death. Satan cannot kill. Only God has the keys to death, hell, and the grave.

So Thankful!

That afternoon found us at the University of Liberia, Fendell Campus. Thousands of fleeing people had taken refuge there that week and no vacant rooms were available on the main campus. We were told however that we could occupy a three room unit close to the main highway linking Kakata and Monrovia.

This was the first time we had the opportunity to eat since we left Monrovia. It was not a scrumptious meal, but it was better than nothing. We had some water also, even though it was not water that was fit to drink.

We were greatly concerned about Ellen and the child she carried inside her. Without proper nourishment, we feared for both of their lives.

The apartment where we stayed that night belonged to a man who had just been beheaded. We spent all that night lying awake in fear while the warriors came in and out of our apartment.

In the morning, I took some clean clothes from the dead man's closet and put them on. Today was July 11th, our second son, Chris's birthday. My wife remembered the date so well. She broke down and cried, saying, "Oh Lord, today is my son's birthday and I don't even know where he is."

Then the Lord impressed upon my mind, that we should leave the area because there was an approaching danger. I informed my little group about the message I had from the Lord, but they all felt a day's delay wouldn't hurt. They were wrong. The campus came under attack from General Prince Johnson of the breakaway Independent National Patriotic Front of Liberia.

Our little group fled from the campus and ran into the nearby forest. We soon reached a flooded creek. We were surrounded by sounds of guns and fighting. The only way of escape was to jump into the creek and swim across it. By now there was shooting everywhere and people were running through the woods. Sadly, there were some children who drowned in that swiftly running creek.

By nightfall, all of us were very exhausted, hungry, and wet. We soon came across a small village where the people knew very little about the war. Our story seemed strange to them. We spent a very uncomfortable night with no help from the people in that village.

The next day, July 12th, we spent the night in Number 7, a plantation belonging to the Firestone Company. I decided while I was there, that I would visit the Todee Mission from which we had fled two months prior. When I arrived at the missions, it was like a ghost town. To my surprise, everything that belonged to us was completely intact.

I made the return trip rather hurriedly with the hope of taking our group back to the mission for temporary settlement, but it was not to be. When I returned from that four hour journey on foot, I found that my wife was gone. The NPFL high command in the area had taken all the women and children in a truck to Kakata. All the men were told to walk. The plan was intended to eliminate as many civilian men as possible.

As I started walking, one of the rebels grabbed me and threatened to kill me. A minister friend, who was traveling with me, interceded with the man and begged him to spare my life. It was approaching four o'clock when I was finally allowed to continue my journey. I was feeling very exhausted and hungry.

We arrived at the Booker T. Washington Institute about 6:30PM. The gatekeeper informed us that it was now curfew hour and that we must spend the night on the campus.

"But I need to find my wife and my friends," I protested.

"No! You can go no further. All the roads are closed. You will have to spend the night at the Institute."

All my protests were to no avail, so I went inside and slept.

I awoke the next day feeling refreshed physically but quite anxious to locate my family. I told the man at the gate that I was leaving and he allowed me to go.

I took a shortcut to reach the yard of the church meeting place in Kakata. How relieved I was to find my wife and friends waiting for me along with another wonderful surprise. My son, Edwin, was there waiting for me also. It was the first time I had seen him since he had been separated from us.

How elated I was to be reunited with him, although I was shocked at how thin and malnourished he looked.

"We have news from Chris and Elijah also," my wife told me with a big smile. "They are staying with Minister Ernest Dahn in Bong Mines. They are both alive and well." Bong Mines was a mining town about forty miles from Kakata. We rejoiced and thanked God who had protected all of us from death.

We remained in Kakata a few days, resting and trying to locate friends and other family members. On one of these occasions, I spotted some white missionaries from the radio station near Monrovia. They too were fleeing for their lives and had made a temporary stopover in Kakata to obtain some needed travel documents. Their intention was to escape to the Ivory Coast.

I walked over and greeted them, asking how they were faring. I introduced myself as a minister of the Gospel of Jesus Christ who was active with the United Pentecostal Church of Liberia.

One of the ladies responded with enthusiasm. "Then you must know Reverend Albert Stewart."

"Yes, of course. He is my father in the Lord."
"I know him also," the lady said.

"Have you any news about him?" I inquired anxiously. "We are afraid he and his children may have been killed in the attack on Monrovia."

"No, they are safe," the missionary informed me. "There was so much fighting in their area that they were forced to stay indoors for seventeen days. They ran out of water and food."

"And what happened to them?" I interrupted, fearing the news would be bad.

"Finally, when they were becoming very weak, they prayed a desperate prayer to God for help. It was then that it occurred to Brother Stewart that he had recently purchased a water bed for his daughters. Not being very knowledgeable about water beds, he had failed to add the proper chemicals to the water."

"Yes," I prodded, "So what happened?"

"They emptied the water from the bed and had enough to drink for several days!"

I gave a shout of joy at the report of this amazing miracle.

"The Lord was faithful to his Word. He kept them alive and they were finally able to find safety in the American Embassy," the missionary continued.

That was the news I wanted to hear. "Thank God!

46

He has done it again, even in the midst of this furnace of fire."

There was so much to be thankful for on that day, in spite of the uncomfortable circumstances all around us. Soon a plan began forming in my mind. It was time to stop cowering in fear. It was time to take this war out of the hands of the devil. We were about to go on the offensive for the Lord.

48

Revelation 1:18

*I am He that liveth, and was dead;
and, behold, I am alive
for evermore, Amen; and have the
keys of hell and of death.*

Conquerors

God began to speak to me about the many lost souls trapped by the war. What if they didn't ever have a chance to go to a church and be saved? What would their fate be? The burden hung over me like a rain cloud.

Sunday morning came, and I was still deciding on a plan. Well armed men roamed the vicinity in droves. Only a few church doors were still open.

Finally I spoke to Brother Mulbah, one of our faithful ministers. "This is the right time for us to plant a church in Kakata. It will be the Conquerors United Pentecostal Church."

This had been a long time dream of both of us up until the war began. Brother Mulbah agreed that the time was right.

We found some chairs and began setting them out on the porch of the house where we were staying. "What are you doing?" one of the soldiers asked me.

"We're getting ready to have church."

"You're crazy!" the soldier retorted.

"I know it," I answered with joy in my heart. The devil hadn't succeeded in killing me and now it was my turn.
We began walking around in the streets singing and

inviting people to the service. Thirty-two people showed up on that porch to have church. Of course there was a much larger audience watching from the street. We started singing:

> What a mighty God we serve,
> What a mighty God we serve,
> Angels bow before Him,
> Heaven and earth adore Him,
> What a mighty God we serve!

We sang and preached as the power of God fell. The people were worshiping God, speaking in tongues, and dancing before the Lord.

Though it was a time of war, the Gospel continued to go forth to all who would dare to listen. The little church grew rapidly as more and more hungry souls were baptized in Jesus name and filled with the Holy Ghost.

Instead of dead bodies, there were people being born again. The war looked like a gigantic funeral, but God turned it into a revival.

God said to me, "This is why I didn't take you out of the war in the first place. I wanted to use you. All the preachers are gone. Some are dead. I preserved you to be a witness unto me."

"I'm sorry, God," I humbly answered. "I'm sorry for not trusting you."

God's power is not limited to good times. While it is true that God is the Prince of Peace, He also remains the God of war and the Captain of our salvation.

In spite of all the adverse circumstances, the church continued to grow. Today, Conquerors United Pentecostal Church has a congregation of 350 people, a fine building, and a beautiful high school. It stands as a witness to the power of the Fourth Man who brought revival in the midst of the fire.

Conquerors Church in Kakata

54

Ellen  10

I shall forever be thankful for Ellen. She has been God's gift to this preacher.

I first met Ellen at the mission school in Fassima. We were attracted to each other immediately, but I was a long way from being ready to settle down. I had plans to travel to America where I would study at Gateway College of Evangelism in St. Louis.

Before leaving, we had a long conversation.

"As you know, I am leaving Liberia, Ellen. I will be gone for four years."

"I will miss you very much," she answered.

"We will pray about this very much. When I come back from America in four years, if you have been faithful and still love me, we will get married."

Throughout my time in America, we wrote letters back and forth to each other. Although there were many girls in America who were friendly to me, I was advised that these girls would have a very difficult time being a good preacher's wife in Liberia.

And so I waited on the Lord and I waited for Ellen.

Four years later, I boarded a plane and headed for home, with my theological degree packed safely in my suitcase. As the plane landed, I looked anxiously out the door to see if anyone was there to meet me. I spotted missionary Jimmy Hall and some of the other ministers waiting for me to arrive. Standing nearby was my beautiful faithful Ellen.

Soon we were married. She gave birth to three strong boys. Now here she was in the midst of a horrible war, getting ready to give birth to another child.

At the same time, Ellen and I were anxious to make contact with our two boys who were living in Bong Mines with Minister Ernest Dahn. There was no car available or public transportation system in any part of the rebel controlled area. The only vehicles available were those that the rebels had confiscated from the people who originally owned them.

One morning I was able to locate a truck that the rebels had looted from the Firestone Plantation Company. It was heading toward Bong Mines. We offered them a small amount of money to take us with them. Since we had so little money, they refused. We began begging them for help.

Suddenly one of the rebel soldiers spotted my sister-in-law, Elsie, and grabbed her. "This one will be my wife," he declared.

Ellen burst into tears and I became very angry. "Please," Ellen begged. "Let my sister alone. She is my mother's last child and if you take her away, my mother will never forgive me. Please, I beg of you. Let my sister go."

For some unknown reason, the soldier let go of Elsie and the rebels agreed to let us ride in the back of the truck.

The road was unpaved and very rough. We were sitting on the floor of the truck along with the rebels in a very miserable state. It was especially difficult for Ellen who was close to her time of delivery.

When the road became too rough for Ellen to sit on the floor, I allowed her to hang on to my arm while I held tightly to an iron bar that I was sitting under.

After an arduous trip, we arrived at Bong Mines, where we were happily reunited with our two boys, Christian and Elijah. How pleased we were to see that they were both doing very well, in spite of the terrible crisis they too had endured. God had protected them, just as He had protected Ellen and me.

But what about the child she had been carrying since this war began? Was it possible that Ellen could give birth to a normal child after all she had been through?

When we reached Bong Mines we were welcomed by Elder Morris who pastored a church in that area. Brother Stephen Benda and his family invited us to stay in their home.

On October 16th, 1990, it came time for our baby to be delivered. There were several mid-wives in Bong Mines who were members of the Pentecostal Church. They agreed to help my wife deliver the baby. Rebecca Galary was the head nurse in the group.

We stood outside the door and listened to a very beautiful sound coming from inside that delivery room. The women were all praying in tongues only minutes before the baby arrived.

As I stood outside the door, I was nervously wondering what would be the outcome of this delivery. Ellen had suffered so much. She had endured long journeys on foot without proper nourishment and with very little water. Many times there was no comfortable bed for her to sleep on and there was no medical care available. The deprivations had been extreme. Was it possible that she could now give birth to a healthy child? We knew the chances were slim.

And so we waited and prayed.

And then it happened. We heard the plaintive cry of a newborn baby echoing throughout the house. Soon someone called to me, "Brother Yarsiah, you are the father of a beautiful baby girl."

I wept for joy. The baby was entirely whole and healthy and Ellen was lively and happy.

As they placed our new arrival in my arms, I looked up to heaven with thanksgiving and cried, "Lord this is truly a miracle of God. This child shall be called *Miracle!*

Not only did God preserve us *from* the fire, He also gave us our Miracle *in* the fire.

Our family
Top row: Edwin Jr., Elijah, Chris
Bottom row: Edwin Sr., Miracle, Ellen

62

Jeremiah 42:10-12

If ye will abide in this land,

Then will I build you,

And not pull you down,

And I will plant you,

And not pluck you up:

For I repent me of the evil that I

have done unto you.

Be not afraid of the king of Babylon,

Of whom ye are afraid,

Be not afraid of him, saith the Lord.

For I am with you to save you,

And to deliver you from his hand.

And will shew mercies unto you,

That he may have mercy upon you,

And cause you to return unto your own land.

Revival in the Fire

The story of the Civil War in Liberia did not end on an ugly note. God took the ugliness and turned it into something very beautiful.

One day as I was sitting under a small bush shelter I had prepared to protect my family from the rain, the Lord began speaking to me. The Lord showed me through the events in Jeremiah chapter 42, that we were not to run from the war. I decided to obey the voice of God which came to me from the pages of the prophet Jeremiah.

We returned to Kakata from Bong Mines in early 1991 in order to pastor the growing congregation that we had founded. God impressed me with the idea of hosting a crusade. It was wartime. There were no schools open, no hospitals open, and very few churches open. There was nothing for the people to do and no place to go. What a perfect time to have a revival! We called it *Kakata for Christ Crusade.*

Kakata, which was known as the educational city of Liberia, was about to experience the mighty power of God. Thousands of people came to the services each night. Altogether, there was an attendance of over 8000. People were standing everywhere to witness these revival meetings. The streets were full and some were standing on the top of cars and on buildings to get a better view.

Many of those who attended the services were members of the fighting forces. Some of them surrendered their hearts to God. When this happened, they began laying down their arms and refusing to fight. These conversions stirred up a lot of anger against us, but we just kept on preaching.

One night a man who owned a disco bar came to the services. The Lord touched his heart and he was baptized and received the Holy Ghost. Afterwards, he went back to his disco and took it all apart. Then he brought all of the musical instruments from the bar to the crusade and gave them to the church.

A young pregnant lady came forward one night during the service. "I have been carrying this baby for over ten months, and haven't been able to give birth. Please pray that God will touch me."

The evangelist turned to her and said, "Young lady, before this crusade ends on Friday, you will have your baby." And that is exactly what happened. The baby arrived to the great joy of everyone who knew the story.

God blessed that meeting with many souls born into the kingdom of God. The church continued to grow. But in 1992 we were once more forced to flee from Kakata.

The Flying Demons

For about a year, Liberia was divided into two sub-political segments known as Monrovia and Greater Liberia. The forces led by Charles Taylor controlled the greater portion of the country while the government of National Unity covered the Monrovia area and its surroundings.

The division seemed strange to most of us, since Liberia has always been thought of as one nation indivisible. We couldn't believe it had happened almost overnight. The reality, however, was that no one could move freely from any of the areas called Greater Liberia into Monrovia or vice versa.

Thus we lost contact with the church in Monrovia. When people asked about Edwin Yarsiah Forkpa, they reported, "He is missing and we presume he is dead."

It was shocking to see how swiftly events had snowballed. We now found ourselves with two different governments in the same country.

Tension began developing between the two administrations. The next thing we realized was that the main highway leading to Monrovia from Gbarnga where Charles Taylor was headquartered was closed. Soon we experienced an embargo on Greater Liberia. The atmosphere became tense to a breaking point.

As civilians, we sensed that something strange was in the air although we had no knowledge of what it was. We prayed that God would save us from whatever was coming.

The neighboring countries of West Africa sent in peace keeping forces in an attempt to bring calmness to the region. Charles Taylor, however, resisted. He had a very strong rebel fighting force.

To drive Charles Taylor's rebels from the area, they sent in jet bombers. These "peace keepers" began dropping bombs everywhere.

One Saturday night, we noticed some very strange movements around Kakata. The spirit of war had resurrected and apparently all hell had broken loose in Monrovia. It was "Operation Octopus," a military campaign by the NPFL to overrun the area and to seize power. And so they conducted an air raid on the inhabitants of Greater Liberia.

It was on a Sunday morning at about six o'clock that the Alpha jet bombers visited us in Kakata for the first time. I had just awakened to prepare for my morning prayer when the small city began to rattle with the vibrating sound of jet bombers. It rained terror and sent us all into a state of turmoil.

Some people hid themselves in the flower bushes, while others ran to the nearby forest. There was much confusion everywhere. Fighters were often running in the same direction as non-fighters.

The Alpha Jets came in pairs. They wreaked massive destruction on everything in their paths in just a matter of minutes. I coined a special name for them: the flying demons.

At dawn every day, we crept under bushes amid mosquitoes and flies so that we could avoid being hit by the bombs. These flying demons seemed to have an uncanny knowledge of our hiding places. We became as bush animals, barely surviving from day to day.

We were getting so hungry, that one day I decided I would go back to our home in Kakata. We had a little food in our house, and I wanted to retrieve it. Miracle was still a small baby and all of us were desperately in need of nourishment.

When I arrived, I found that a rebel commander had moved into our house. He had taken over everything we owned.

"What are you doing here?" the commander questioned me.

"This is my house," I said. "I live here."

"Not any more you don't," he answered. "This is not your house any more."

"What are you talking about? This is my place and my wife and my children want to get in here."

But it was no use arguing with the man. I found some of our church friends, and managed to get just a very small amount of food to take back with me.

As I headed back into the forest to find my family, something kept urging me, "Hurry up! Hurry up!" So I did. As I hurried toward the camp where my family stayed, I saw two jet bombers flying right toward the place in the forest where I had left my family. I couldn't believe it!

Little did I know that the place we had chosen to stay, was actually a military camp. When I reached the camp, there was no one there. I began calling for my family.

Finally I spotted Edwin. I ran to him and cried, "Where's your mother?"

"I don't know," he answered. We frantically began looking for the rest of the family. Finally we spotted Ellen and the other three children. I uttered a great sigh of relief.

We were warned that the bombers would be back. So at 4:00 AM, while it was still dark, we began moving again. We had to walk through a creek for a long way. Finally, we arrived at a place where we rested and tried to hide from the enemy. We began to pray and soon God spoke to me.

"This place is called the secret place of the most high!" He said to me. We were greatly comforted.

We headed toward a village where we thought there would be no fighting. When we arrived there, we saw people lying everywhere. Many of them were injured and bleeding. Some were dying.

"Won't you please help us?" they cried.

It was a hard thing to do, but we had to tell them: "How can we help you? We have no food or medicine. We cannot help you." And we kept on walking.

Finally we made a new plan. I knew a friend of mine in that area that had an old bus. The bus had a little gas in it. So we prayed and then we took the whole family and drove and drove. After some time, we arrived at a place that would indeed be the secret place of the most high. It was a place called Gibi. There we found a little bit of "normal" living for the months to come.

In Gibi, we joined with Bishop Joseph Garway of the Apostolic Alliance Mission. Bishop Garway was with another church organization; however he had attended Bible School at Christian Life College in Stockton, California, led by Pastor Kenneth Haney, and he believed the Apostolic message just as we did.

We began to preach and once again we experienced revival as more and more people were baptized in Jesus' name and filled with the Holy Ghost. It was miracle time once more!

After we had been in Gibi for about seven months, the rebels learned that I was in the area preaching. They came to the mission demanding to see me.

When I heard they were coming, I left the mission and ran into the forest. The rebels stayed for several hours. Finally they took a few things and left. I waited in the forest until late in the night, and then slipped back into the mission station.

The Lord seemed to be urging me to move on for the safety of my family.

Before these events happened, I had received news from a town called Totota. This was a place where Christians of many denominations had gone to find safety. The majority of these people were Pentecostals and they had requested that I come and pastor them.

After prayer, God directed me to leave Gibi and move my family to Totota.

Trapped! 13

It was only God's provision that kept us alive during those days of war. Many people all around us were dying of disease and malnutrition. It was the Lord's mighty hand that kept us strong for the work He had given us to do.

While we were in Gibi, once again we were in need of some food to keep us alive. So every evening some of the men in the church would go out in the forest and set animal traps.

Every morning they would go and check the traps, and every morning there would be some small animals in the traps. We would clean the animals, season them, and cook them. The meat from these animals kept us from starving to death.

But after a while, the animals got smart and learned to avoid the traps. One morning we went to check and there was nothing in the traps. We prayed for a miracle and set the traps again that evening.

The next morning, the men went out to check the traps again. Sure enough there was something to eat waiting for us. It was a big black cobra!

What did we do? We cleaned the cobra, seasoned it, cooked it, and blessed it. The meat was delicious.

I can give you this miraculous report. Every one in my family came through those terrible times strong and healthy.

God was our provider.

Fourth Man in the Cell

We said our thanks and good-bys to the Garways who had shown us such kind hospitality for seven months. Then we left the AA Mission with our four children, traveling in the direction the Lord was leading us. Once again we were trusting Him to lead us as we stepped into the unknown.

We had no doubt about our decision whatsoever, regardless of the warnings that came from well meaning friends who advised us concerning the frequent visits of the *flying demons*. We knew we were in the will of God; however, we had no way of anticipating the opposition we would experience in the near future.

Our family traveled through the jungle for seven difficult hours and arrived in Totota the following day.

Upon accepting the responsibility of pastoring the group in Totota in 1992, revival came. Once more we began to witness a mighty move of God as more and more people came to know the Lord in the power of His Spirit. The church grew. We decided to call our new congregation *The Upper Room United Pentecostal Church.*

As soon as we settled down to pastor this church that was made up of displaced people, the devil used the rebel police and soldiers under the command of General Isaac Musa to usher in our next trial by fire.

The rebels got word that I was preaching in the area. They were not happy with the rapid growth of our church and they came looking for me. This time, they seized both Ellen and me right in front of our four children.

Our children were crying. They wondered what was to become of their mother and father.

The rebels threw us in a jail that was filthy, dark, and smelly. There was another man in the same cell as we were. We had to be very careful where to step, because the floor was covered with filth. As we were wondering what would become of us and our children, we were unexpectedly joined by a fourth person.

The man spoke with authority in his voice. "Who are you and why are you in this jail?" he asked us.

"I am a pastor and this is my wife. We were arrested for preaching the message of repentance which included condemning the killing of innocent children and civilians by the rebels. They found us on a road where a man had died of starvation. They are accusing us of being responsible for the man's death."

When I said that, the man went into a rage. He screamed, "It's not right to cast an innocent man of God and his wife in jail. I promise you that I will see that the rebels release you unconditionally."

75

He began hollering and banging on the door until a guard finally came and took him into an office. "You must let these people go. He is a man of God and you have no right to put him in jail!" he said in a loud voice.

For some reason they listened to this man and obeyed him. To our great joy, the authorities came, opened the prison door, and freed us.

When we were reunited with our family, the children were very upset. Elijah, my youngest boy said to me, "When I grow up I'm going to become a soldier, and I will kill everybody."

"Well, Elijah, you don't have the Holy Ghost yet, or you wouldn't say such things," I said to him. "God has taken care of us one more time and we should be very thankful."

The man responsible for our release disappeared and we never saw him again. We never knew his name. We could only conclude that once again we had been delivered by the Fourth One in that cell.

Ellen & Edwin Yarsiah
Prisoners of War

Acts 2:38

Then Peter said unto them,
Repent and be baptized everyone of
you in the name of Jesus Christ
for the remission of sins,
And you shall receive
the gift of the Holy Ghost

Salvation 15

After being delivered from jail, we were more determined than ever that we would preach in spite of the efforts of Satan to destroy us.

Even though it was dangerous to travel far into the interior for any reason, we decided to obey the Lord and carry the Gospel to the dying people of Bong County. How could they hear without a preacher?

Our message of Bible salvation was repentance, baptism in the name of the Lord Jesus Christ for the remission of sins, and the baptism of the Holy Ghost with the initial sign of speaking in tongues as the Spirit gives the utterance.

The Bong County area of Liberia had been settled by the Lutherans in the early 1940's. The full message of Bible salvation had not yet been preached there.

One day someone told me that the Holy Ghost could never fall on people in Bong County because of previous teaching by those who had earlier evangelized this area. To this person I said, "Stand by and watch."

One evening during the service, a lady in the congregation broke the silence and began speaking in other tongues for the first time. That was the beginning of a real revival as one person after another received this beautiful experience.

80

Then one evening, we asked the people who were hungry for God to form a line. We began laying hands on them and praying for them to be filled with the Holy Ghost. As I was praying, one of the altar workers came to me and said, "Brother Yarsiah, come see for yourself. Your son, Edwin is at the end of the line and he is speaking in tongues."

I rushed to where Edwin was praying, and was filled with rapturous exuberance. Then I looked over and saw my second son, Chris. He too was being filled with the Holy Ghost. Once more I was overwhelmed by the goodness of our God.

This wave of Apostolic revival swept across the schoolyard where the crusade was being hosted as crowds of people came pouring in to see what was happening. God was confirming His Word.

The crusade team under my leadership moved further into the interior part of Bong with a fifty man team singing:

> *I do not worry anymore,*
> *I prayed to Jesus and He answered my prayer,*
> *I do not worry anymore.*

We traveled on foot down jungle paths and through villages for four hours, singing as we walked. We had to pass through rebel checkpoints and answer all kinds of questions about who we were and where we were going. Finally we reached Saniyea, a very beautiful town in Bong County.

That night the main street through the town was a sight to behold. Our crusade team members were joined by townspeople who were hungry for God. Soon we were joined by rebel soldiers with their A-K 47 rifles hanging on them. We all walked around the town singing together and praising the Lord for several hours. The music was beautiful!

The service drew a crowd from all around as we preached the Gospel of Jesus that night. Some of the soldiers came and confessed their sins, asking for prayer.

The crusade lasted for nine days. By the end, we had baptized thirty people including a member of the Jehovah's Witness church, William W. Miller and his entire family. We explained to him that the Jehovah of the Old Testament is Jesus of the New Testament.

Brother Miller and his family followed our fifty man crusade team back to Totota. Later, God called him to preach the Gospel and he and his family became valuable assets in the kingdom of God.

It was the beginning of another new church planted right on the front lines of the war. With death and destruction everywhere, we decided to call this *The New Life Pentecostal Church.*

The Maimu Call

One day I received a call from an elderly woman named Gweh Briggs who was living in a nearby town called Maimu. "Please come to Maimu and help us," she pleaded.

Her call for help reminded me so strongly of the vision Paul had in Acts the 17th chapter. In that vision, a man appeared to him from Macedonia, saying, "Come over into Macedonia and help us."

> *Acts 16:10 And after he had seen the vision, immediately we endeavored to go into Macedonia, assuredly gathering that the Lord had called us for to preach the gospel unto them.*

When I received the call from Maimu, I felt a strong need to go.

This lady had received the Holy Ghost in 1950. She needed to be baptized and she needed instruction in the Word of God.

Our Gospel team left Totota and walked about one hour down the highway leading to Monrovia until we reached the town of Maimu. We conducted our first service on the ladies porch. The presence of the Lord was strong in that house as we prayed and worshiped God and preached the message of salvation. Soon we baptized Sister Briggs and a number of other people in Maimu. It was the beginning of another new church that was born in the fire.

84

We decided we would come back and conduct a crusade in that town. The crusade was successful and many people came to know the Lord in the power of His Spirit.

Later we were given a large tract of land for a church building.

What should we call this new church? The choice seemed apparent to me. This church would be called *The New Macedonian United Pentecostal Church.*

Today the church in Maimu is being pastored by Brother Miller who was converted in our crusade in Saniyea. He is the pastor, his wife leads the choir, and his children are all involved in the work of the Lord.

I remember returning to Maimu for a service some time after the war had ended. In that service, Sister Gweh Briggs stood to give a most unusual testimony.

"I want to thank God for the war," she declared.

We could hardly believe what she was saying. How could anybody thank God for the war?

She continued. "If it were not for this war, I would never have met Brother Yarsiah, and I would not have known the truth of God's Word. Because of the war, we now have a church in Maimu that teaches the truth. I am so thankful for what God did for us in the midst of the war." We joined her in this very strange praise. We thanked God for the war.

God had indeed worked in mysterious ways, his wonders to perform.

87

One day I received a call from Gbarnga, the city where Charles Taylor was headquartered. There was a group of people there whose pastor had fled to Ghana to escape the fighting. They requested that I come and minister to them.

So some of us traveled to Gbarnga to be of assistance in reorganizing the church in that city. Once again, God greatly blessed our efforts.

One day while we were there, God began talking to me about trying to reconnect with the church in Monrovia. It had been four years since we had been forced to leave the capital city. Reports had circulated among the saints in Monrovia that Brother Edwin Yarsiah had been killed by the rebels.

"I feel God wants me to make contact with Brother Stewart and the churches in Monrovia," I told some of the saints.

"How will you get there?" someone asked.

"I don't know, but I need to go," I answered.

God settled that question for me.

While we had been ministering in Totota, there was a radio station from which the rebels were broadcasting. I decided that it was an excellent opportunity to spread the Gospel. So I was given permission to preach the Word of God over that radio station.

One day someone from Fassama turned on the radio and heard me preaching over the air waves. They shared the news with Brother Stewart and the saints in Monrovia. "Brother Yarsiah is not dead. I heard him preaching the Gospel on the radio today."

My friends greatly rejoiced at the news. It had been four years since they had heard from me. Everyone assumed I was dead.

Brother Stewart chose a man to drive behind the rebel lines and try to locate me and two other pastors, Brother Kamara, and Brother Gayflor. As God would have it, the three of us were together in Gbarnga.

One morning, just as we were preparing to open our church service in Gbarnga, a car drove up to our meeting house. Out stepped the man who had been sent to find me. What rejoicing there was that day.

I stopped by Totota to tell my family the good news that I was traveling to Monrovia. I well remember the date, because it was on my wife's birthday, May 2nd, 1994. What a birthday surprise!

When we arrived in Monrovia, we had a blessed reunion. After four difficult years, we rejoiced to know that God had delivered us in the midst of the fires of war.

We began reporting all the blessings and miracles God had provided. Brother Stewart and the district board were particularly blessed by the reports of the revivals and the new churches that had been opened. All of us worshiped and praised the Lord for the things He had done.

The district board made plans to follow up on all the new congregations that had been planted. Brother Stewart and I traveled together to the various cities and villages to help strengthen the new saints and to further establish the churches.

At the beginning of the war, our churches in Liberia had an active membership of about 8000. We now have 25,000 active members.

Before the war we had 45 churches and 24 preaching points. After the war, we had 96 churches and 58 preaching points. Prior to the war, we had churches in 6 of the 13 counties of Liberia. Now we have churches in 10 counties and there are plans underway to reach the other 3 counties with the Gospel of Jesus.

Surely this is the fulfillment of the Scripture found in Isaiah 66:8 that says: "... *for as soon as Zion travailed, she brought forth her children.*"

Job 5:20

In famine
he shall redeem thee from death:
and in war
from the power of the sword.

I Am a Witness

My life has been a series of miracles.

I came from the little township of Fassama in the country of Liberia, West Africa. Missionary Pauline Gruse started a mission station there in the year 1952. She preached the Gospel of salvation to the people in the area and gave them some basic education.

It was while attending the Fassima Mission School that I came to know the Lord personally.

In 1977, I was blessed to be able to travel to America to continue my education at Gateway College of Evangelism in St. Louis, Missouri. I graduated after four years with a Bachelor of Arts degree in Theology. I later received a Master of Arts Degree in Theology from Cypress Bible College in Van, Texas.

Toward the end of my studies at Gateway College of Evangelism, I penned these words:

> *Since my arrival in the United States, I have had several opportunities that could have paved the way for me to stay in America. But as Brother Paul heard a call, I too have heard: "Come back to Africa and help us."*

I have read it in letters from friends at home, missionaries have told me, and the Lord himself has told me many times while on my knees. Day and night I remember being in that African village seven years ago where the people cried, "We have never heard the name of Jesus' once in our whole lives. Please come back and help us."

Now that most of my schooling is over, I look to the future. What next? Once again the Apostle Paul comes to my mind: "I have fought a good fight, I have finished my course, I have kept the faith . . ." I will return to my own people to labor in the Lord's vineyard.

Lord you have taken me through it all. Now here I am. Send me.

When I returned to my beloved country of Liberia, I struggled to find my place in the work of the Lord. Before the war began, I do not feel I was following the perfect plan of God for my life.

But the Lord knew my heart. God saw my heart and considered me worthy to carry His message to the many Liberians who needed salvation so desperately.

God chose the vehicle of the Liberian Civil War to put me in the exact place He wanted me at exactly the right time. He gave me a Godly wife and family to help me and the strength of the Holy Ghost to sustain me.

No matter what God asks you to endure, if you obey Him, your life will be enriched by the experience. Remember—gold is never destroyed by fire. He said, *"Lo I am with you alway, even unto the end of the world" (Matthew 28:20).*

You can count on Him. He will be the *Fourth Man in your fire* and He will never fail you. I am a witness.

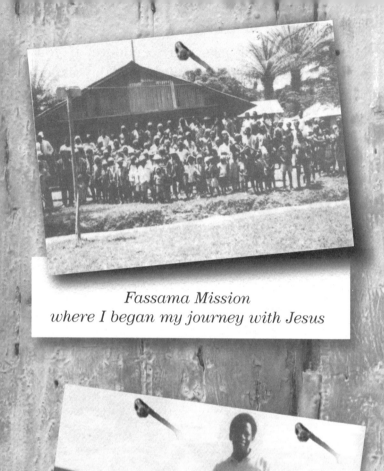

Fassama Mission
where I began my journey with Jesus

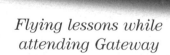

Flying lessons while
attending Gateway

My graduation from Gateway College of Evangelism

Edwin Yarsiah delivering the salutatory address in the high school graduation at Monrovia City Hall in 1977.

Co-authors Edwin Yarsiah
& Judith Bentley

About the co-author. . .

Judith Bentley resides in Dexter, Missouri with her husband, Pastor Robert Bentley. They are both prolific writers, having made many contributions to Sunday School literature, periodicals, and books.

Judith has a B.S. in Education and has taught in public and private schools for thirty five years. She has ministered and taught in England, Scotland, Russia, Estonia, Kazakhstan, and the Ukraine as well as extensively in the USA.

She is the daughter of Reverend and Mrs. Stanley Chambers, the mother of three daughters, Melanie Nordstrom, Roberta Crawford, and Kristin Hoover, and a grandmother of eight.

Her favorite hobby is writing. Her books include:

The Russian Series:
Moscow Mornings
Red September
Red Star, White Nights
Dancing With the Bear

Ship Ahoy! The Life & Times
of Stanley & Catherine Chambers

I've Just Started Living,
Priscilla McGruder's incredible story
*   of deliverance from cancer*

These books may be purchased at:

Bentley Educational Ministries
11375 Northview Drive
Dexter, MO 63841
Ph. 575.624.1890

To purchase additional copies of
Fourth Man In The Fire contact:

Reverend Edwin Yarsiah Forkpa
c/o Joyce Moore
208 Bittersweet Dr.
O'Fallon, MO 63366
Ph. 636.272.6384

Other writings by Edwin Yarsiah Forkpa include:

He Rescued Me
Twelve Reasons Why You Need the
  Baptism of the Holy Ghost